Jailane de Souza Aquino
Claudiane M.Q. Medeiros
João A. da Silva

What you need to know about eggs

Jailane de Souza Aquino
Claudiane M.Q. Medeiros
João A. da Silva

What you need to know about eggs

A nutritional and technological overview

ScienciaScripts

Cover image: www.ingimage.com

This book is a translation from the original published under ISBN 978-3-330-76962-5.

Publisher:
Sciencia Scripts
is a trademark of
Dodo Books Indian Ocean Ltd. and OmniScriptum S.R.L publishing group

120 High Road, East Finchley, London, N2 9ED, United Kingdom
Str. Armeneasca 28/1, office 1, Chisinau MD-2012, Republic of Moldova, Europe
Managing Directors: Ieva Konstantinova, Victoria Ursu
info@omniscriptum.com

Printed at: see last page
ISBN: 978-620-8-62641-9

SUMMARY

SUMMARY

Eggs, especially hens' eggs, are a low-cost food rich in nutrients that are important for human health, such as lipids, proteins and vitamins. Egg proteins contain peptides with various functions such as antimicrobial, antiviral, antioxidant, antidiabetic, immunostimulant, anticancer and antihypertensive. However, eggs require adequate microbiological control as they are one of the main sources of *Salmonella sp*. Research into methods to improve their integrity or to maintain their quality during storage is intense. A great deal of research has been carried out with the aim of developing suitable techniques to reduce the microbial load of eggs, including ultra-pasteurization and pasteurization treatments, etc. Dehydration methods such as *freeze-drying* and *spray-drying* have been used by industries because they offer greater microbiological safety, ease of transportation, less storage space and greater stability during storage. The nutritional, functional and sensory value of eggs has favored their use in the food industry. However, preservation techniques can influence oxidation reactions, as well as protein quality, which can lead to a reduction in nutritional value and organoleptic characteristics. Therefore, analyzing the protein and lipid quality of eggs and egg products is an important aspect, as these parameters refer to bioavailability or the ability to metabolically provide available amino acids and fatty acids necessary for the various functions of the human body.

CHAPTER 1

EGGS: CHARACTERIZATION, NUTRITIONAL IMPORTANCE AND MICROBIOLOGICAL

Claudiane Magliano Queiroz Medeiros; Thais Helena Figueirêdo do Bonfim; Joâo Andrade da Silva, Jailane de Souza Aquino

CHARACTERIZATION

The name 'egg' refers to eggs that come from hens; when they come from other species, the origin must be indicated. It is a food and food ingredient that is widely consumed and accepted in many cultures, with hen's eggs being the most widely consumed. Eggs are one of the main foods in the human diet, with the advantage of being low cost and providing essential nutrients for the functioning of the body, being substantially important in regions of nutritional vulnerability. Their average annual consumption is 200 units per capita, with China being the world's largest producer (PISKORSKA-PLISZCZYNSKA et al. 2014; CONRAD et al. 2017).

Egg formation begins in the bird's ovary, where layers of fats and proteins are added to form the yolk. Then, in the oviduct, the egg white is added, with the chalazas being the first to be formed, as they have the function of supporting the yolk centrally in the egg, then albumin is secreted by the cells lining this organ. In the uterus, water and mineral salts are added to the egg white and, finally, the shell is formed with calcium carbonate and other proteins. The egg shell is a porous structure made up of calcium, phosphorus and other trace minerals whose concentrations are influenced by the birds' diet. The shell has the role of protecting the egg from external damage and keeping the internal contents adequately protected from loss to the outside environment. In addition, the minerals present in the shell are required to aid the development of the embryo, and the porosity is an indispensable factor for embryonic respiration (KETTA & TUMOVA, 2016; IANNOTTI et al. 2014).

The egg white is rich in proteins and mineral salts, and alternates thick and thin layers of albumen, an essential characteristic for hindering the movement of microorganisms.

The protein content is of high biological value, an important source of essential amino acids and selenium. Around it, the egg white is contained by the testaceous membranes that coat the egg internally and form the air chamber, which is formed at the time of laying, when the temperature difference from inside to outside the bird's body causes the membrane in direct contact with the egg white to retract, while the membrane in contact with the shell remains unchanged. The air chamber is formed in the space between them, which increases as the egg ages (IANNOTTI et al 2014).

The yolk is an emulsion of fat in water, rich in triglycerides, phospholipids and cholesterol, most of which are unsaturated fatty acids. It also contains choline and proteins, the latter of which are probably involved in the primary nutrition of the embryo, although they are also involved in the emulsifying, antimicrobial and antioxidant capacities of the yolk. High-density lipoproteins are responsible for antioxidant functions and antimicrobial activity, and we also find a high vitamin content such as vitamins A, E, D, B12 and folate, among others, as well as the minerals phosphorus, potassium and calcium, with the composition of the yolk being strongly influenced by the bird's diet. The yolk is surrounded by a membrane called vitelline which has the function of containing its components (IANNOTTI et al., 2014). Figure 1 shows the structures of the egg and the respective nutritional content of the white and yolk.

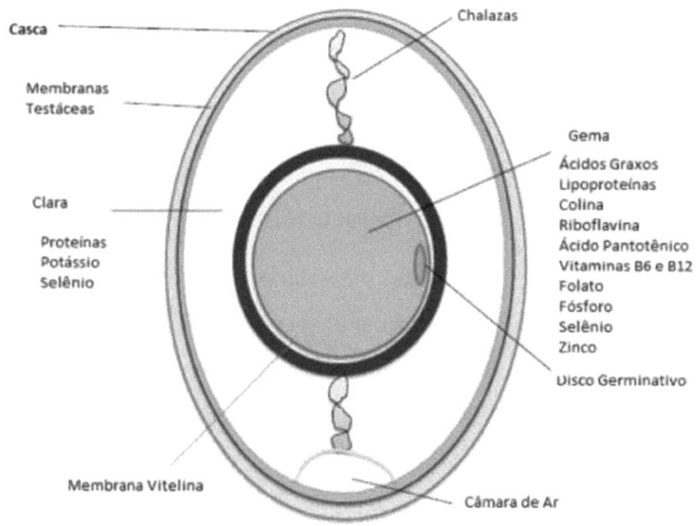

Figure 1 - Egg components and nutrients found in egg white and yolk. Adapted from Iannotti et al, 2014.

According to Brazilian legislation, eggs are classified into groups, classes and types. The classification by group corresponds to the color of the shell. Eggs in the 'white' group are those whose shells are white or whitish, and those whose shells are reddish are classified in the 'colored' group. The color of the rind is not directly related to its nutritional content, but only to the breed of bird (BRASIL, 1965).

Qualitatively, they can be divided into classes A, B and C, the first of which corresponds to those with a clean, undeformed shell, a fixed air chamber, a clear and transparent egg white with intact calazas, a translucent, intact yolk and no microbial development. Class B eggs are those with characteristics similar to those described for class A eggs, however, they may have discreet spots and deformations on the shell and slightly off-center and deformed yolks, but without the development of microorganisms. Type C allows for defects in texture, spots and contours on the shells, cloudy whites, decentralized and deformed yolks, slightly cloudy whites , but with intact calazas and no microbial development (BRASIL, 1965).

With regard to weight, eggs are classified into types (1, 2, 3 and 4) according to their unit weight or the weight of a dozen, always measured in grams. Type 1, or extra eggs, must weigh at least 60g/unit or 720g/dozen; type 2, or large eggs, must weigh 55g/unit or 660g/dozen; type 3, or medium eggs, weighs 50g/unit or 600g/dozen; and type 4, or small eggs, weighs 45g/unit or 540g/dozen. Brazilian legislation allows types 1, 2 and 3 a tolerance of up to 10% of eggs of the immediately inferior type (BRASIL, 1965).

Eggs that do not meet the class and type parameters are considered unfit for consumption, but can be used industrially without the purpose of human consumption. In Brazil, the Regulations for the Industrial and Sanitary Inspection of Products of Animal Origin (RIISPOA) (2017), define as criteria for prohibition of consumption eggs that show alterations to the yolk and white (including rupture of the vitelline membrane, dark spots or presence of blood, embryo development), dried egg, alterations characteristic of rotting, the presence of fungus, externally or internally, abnormal color, smell or taste, eggs that are dirty externally or have been in contact with substances capable of transmitting strange smells or tastes that could infect them, rupture of the shell and the testis membrane, or when they contain toxic substances (BRASIL, 2006).

The legislation emphasizes that when packing eggs, it is forbidden for eggs from different groups, classes and types to be packed in the same container, nor can eggs of different species be packed in the same volume (BRASIL, 2006).

MICROBIOLOGICAL ASPECTS

Eggs need proper microbiological control because they are one of the main sources of *Salmonellasp,* a pathogenic bacterium whose habitat is the intestines of humans, birds, animals and insects. In many cases, this microorganism can be present in eggs and contaminate preparations; since eggs, meat and their derivatives are reported to be the main carriers of salmonellosis in humans. As one of the most prevalent food-borne diseases, Brazilian legislation has defined that *Salmonellasp* should not be found in 25g or 25 mL of eggs and egg products (BRASIL, 2001; SUTHIENKUL et al, 2012).

Due to the modernization of laying bird management, questions have been raised about the appropriate conditions of the laying environment, comparing traditional and modern techniques and the impact of each on the microbiological load of the shell, especially in terms of the presence of coliforms, aerobic microorganisms, yeasts and moulds. When comparing free-range and caged housing methods, there is an association between greater contamination of the shell when the birds are kept in free-range housing, probably due to the precariousness of the facilities, greater contact with surfaces that are difficult to sanitize or that are not sanitized, or even due to horizontal contamination (from one bird to another). Also in this respect, there is a relationship between the type of shell contamination and the species of chicken, and studies are needed to associate the strain of bird with the most suitable type of housing (JONES; ANDRESON, 2013).

The microbiological contamination of eggs is influenced by extrinsic and intrinsic factors, the former being: the bacterial strain present in the environment, the temperature of the environment, the humidity of the shell, the number of microorganisms present in the shell and the storage conditions. In addition to these, the intrinsic influencing factors are: the degree of porosity and thickness of the peel and the extent of the film covering the peel. Although the strain of bacteria and the initial microbial load have an influence on the degree of penetration of microorganisms inside the egg, washing eggs does not appear to be a technique that prevents their internal contamination, probably due to the damage that sanitizers cause to the film covering the shell, which increases concern about the recontamination of the shell, as washing damages the cuticle, which can facilitate the penetration of microorganisms (SAMIULLAH et al, 2013).

In addition to treatments that seek to reduce the microbial load already contaminating eggs, many scientists have sought to improve commercial vaccines for laying hens in order to prevent contamination of internal tissues and consequently eggs. Vaccines formulated with attenuated *Salmonella* Enteritidis have been tested and compared with traditional vaccines and it has been noticed that, as well as being safe for the birds, there is an increase in antibody production and an improvement in egg production standards. With a more efficient immune response, contamination of internal organs and eggs by *Salmonella* Enteritidis, *the* main strain of *Salmonella* involved in human disease, is reduced. Scientists suggest that one strategy for the interaction between attenuated microorganisms and birds would be to administer this type of vaccine through water or food, with the advantage that there is no need to handle the birds to apply the vaccines individually (NANDRE; MATSUDA; LEE, 2013; JAWALE; LEE 2014).

The search for efficient methods capable of eliminating or even reducing the presence of *Salmonella* Enteritidis in eggs becomes more important as this is the serotype most commonly isolated from eggs and, consequently, the one most involved in human diseases, followed by *Salmonella* Typhimurium. Many studies report that contamination of the internal contents of eggs occurs in two ways: one is related to the ability of the microorganism to penetrate the egg through pores or cracks in the shell, and the second is contamination resulting from internal infestation of the bird, with colonization of the oviduct being the main cause of contamination of eggs during their formation. The greater involvement of *Salmonella Enteritidis in* contaminated eggs may be associated with the greater ease with which this microorganism colonizes the oviduct or its superior ability to survive the egg's antimicrobial system (VAIBHAV et al, 2014).

QUALITY ASPECTS

Egg shape has been shown to be related to quality aspects, especially in terms of grading, as eggs with non-standard shapes tend to receive lower grades and are consequently devalued. Eggs with little symmetry between their width and length fit poorly into egg cartons and tend to break more easily during transportation and storage. The evaluation of the symmetry between width and length is called the shape index, obtained by the formula (width/length)x100. If the result is less than 72 the egg is classified as elongated, results between 72 and 76 classify the egg as standard and those above 76 are considered round eggs (DUMAN et al., 2016).

The ovoscopy test involves subjecting eggs to a beam of light that passes through them and allows the evaluator to observe the integrity of the shell, yolk, white and embryo development, if any. This test is carried out in a darkroom to allow better observation of the results. Satisfactory quality results are: a firm yolk, high viscosity of the white and a well-positioned air chamber, which becomes larger as the egg gets older (BRASIL, 1990).

Another parameter used to assess quality is the Haugh Unit (HU), a method that relates the height or thickness of the egg white to the weight of the egg. The height of the egg white is measured with the egg open on a flat surface. This test can traditionally be done using a micrometer (an object used to measure thickness), but there are several electronic devices on the market that provide complete information after analyzing the open egg, including both the HU and the weight of the white and/or yolk, the color of the yolk and the weight of the egg.

Eggs tend to show lower HU values over the course of storage due to the loss of moisture to the external environment, which reduces the thickness and viscosity of the egg white. Storage temperature has an influence on HU, as it has been shown that eggs stored with or without refrigeration vary in their HU results, which were lower as the eggs were stored longer at 25°C compared to those stored for the same length of time at 7°C. The higher the HU value, the better the quality of the eggs, which are classified as AA (100 to 72), A (71 to 60), B (59 to 30), C (29 to 0) (SURESH et al, 2015).

Immediately after laying, the eggs begin the process of exchanging gases with the external environment. This exchange is necessary for the development of the embryo and at the same time is responsible for the deterioration of the egg. The porosity of the shell leads to loss of CO_2 and evaporation of water if the humidity of the external environment is lower than that inside the egg. This process leads to a change in the lid system, which exists to maintain the balance of gas exchange. With the loss of CO_2 to the external environment, the pH rises and changes are triggered in the gelatinous structure of the egg white, making it more fluid, possibly due to changes in the ovomucin-lizosime complex. At the same time, albumin is gradually and irreversibly transformed into S-ovoalbumin, leading to a loss of its gelling and foaming properties.

The migration of water into the yolk through the vitelline membrane, which is also weakened, leads to a decrease in the height of the yolk, making it flatter. All these changes are considerably influenced by storage time and temperature.

The yolk index and the albumen index are other factors associated with egg quality. The former is obtained from the ratio between yolk diameter and height, with lower results being reported as the egg white loses moisture to the yolk due to the higher osmotic pressure in the yolk, This means that the progressive transfer of water from the albumen to the yolk causes the yolk membrane to weaken, causing the internal contents to liquefy. Values of 0.42 to 0.40 are considered satisfactory for fresh eggs. The albumen index relates the height of the white to the weight of the egg, and this result is also directly related to the loss of CO_2 and water to the external environment during the storage period.

The air chamber is also affected by the processes of CO_2 and humidity loss, which means that there is more space inside for air to enter and the chamber increases. For these reasons, older eggs have larger air chambers and their gravity decreases over time. A practical test for observing the lifespan of an egg is to immerse it in water and observe whether it remains at the bottom of the container or rises to the surface; if it floats, this indicates an enlarged air chamber, i.e. an old egg (YUCEER; CANER, 2013; SURESH et al, 2015).

The quality assessment of the shell should also be taken into account, as problems with this aspect have a direct impact on the economic waste of eggs, since brittle shells make it difficult to market them due to breakage, and there is a high percentage of losses during the production chain, causing losses for producers, while shells with quality problems can also lead to the devaluation of eggs due to the downgrading of the product in terms of its classification. The nutrition of the birds and the advanced age of the layers affect the strength and thickness of the eggshells, with older birds laying eggs with weaker shells.

Recent research has shown that assessing the integrity of the film covering the eggshell is also a parameter for assessing quality, since the greater the damage to this structure, the more susceptible the egg is to microbial attack and loss of moisture to the external environment. For this reason, research is being carried out to find alternative ways of sanitizing eggs. The temperature of the washing water and the concentration of the sanitizer must be monitored, as high washing temperatures are associated with the expansion of internal structures and can result in the rupture of the vitelline membrane. A concentration of 50ppm of chlorinated compounds has been the most suitable for chemically sanitizing eggshells, and should only be used immediately before industrialization processes (YUCEER; CANER, 2013; SURESH et al, 2015; BRASIL, 1965).

NUTRITIONAL IMPORTANCE

Because of their important nutritional content, eggs are considered to be very nutritious foods, as they provide essential amino acids, fatty acids and vitamins as part of their composition, meaning that their consumption generates various health benefits. Shi et al (2011) cite the benefits of egg consumption as its content of monounsaturated fatty acids, minerals, essential amino acids and B vitamins. In addition to these, eggs are also cited as low-calorie foods, sources of folate, ribofavin, selenium, vitamin A and proteins of high biological value (SANTINI et al, 2012). The existence of phytochemicals such as lutein and zeaxanthin in egg yolk may be involved in the prevention of age-related macular degeneration, cataracts and they also have an antioxidant effect (WU et al, 2011). In addition to its richness in nutrients, eggs are a low-cost food and are therefore easily accessible to people with lower purchasing power.

Egg proteins contain peptides with various important biological functions that are being studied all over the world. Among the known functions are antimicrobial, antiviral, antioxidant, antidiabetic, immunostimulant and anticancer, as well as antihypertensive activity (POKORA et al, 2014; LIU et al, 2015). Liu et al (2015) proposed the identification and isolation of peptides with anti-inflammatory action obtained from egg whites and concluded that, *in vitro*, the amino acids aspartate, serine, glutamine, leucine and lysine may play an important role in antioxidant activity. Ren et al (2014) who also investigated antioxidant activity from duck egg peptides concluded that those with acidic, hydrophobic and low molecular weight characteristics expressed better antioxidant potential. Meanwhile, Pokora et al (2014) cite the importance of peptides with antihypertensive activity, since these substances have demonstrated action comparable to that of synthetic drugs, and it is suggested that these peptides be exploited in the pharmaceutical industry.

Furthermore, Jia et al. (2017) found that eggshell membranes, usually waste from production, can help maintain intestinal health by providing low-digestibility proteins with a physiological role similar to that of dietary fiber, stimulating fecal fermentation and improving bacterial flora. In addition, the action of these membranes is also associated with the fight against liver damage, fibrosis and, due to their intestinal benefits, an important factor against intestinal dysbiosis.

The omega-3 fatty acids found in egg yolks are associated with an improved physiological response to cardiovascular diseases, as well as being important for the prevention and treatment of neurological diseases, cancer, obesity, inflammatory diseases, as well as reducing the risk of premature birth and helping to develop visual acuity and cognitive functions in children (IANNOTTI et al., 2014; LEMAHIEU et al., 2013). Considering all these benefits, a lot of research has looked into ways of manipulating the fatty acid content of egg yolks, since the concentration of this nutrient can be modified based on the birds' diet. Lemahieu et al. (2013) proposed adding microalgae to the birds' diet as a way of verifying the increase in omega-3 content in the yolk. This research comes as an alternative to current practices, which generally add fish oil to diets and may transfer the fishy flavor to the egg. As a result, the authors reported an increase in the content of omega-3, especially docosahexaenoic acid (DHA), as well as an increase in the content of carotenoids, which are fat-soluble pigments with anti-inflammatory and antioxidant action.

Lutein and zeaxanthin, which are carotenoids found in egg yolks, are linked to the prevention of diseases such as atherosclerosis, diabetes and degenerative eye diseases such as cataracts. HDL lipoprotein seems to be the main carrier of these carotenoids to the retina. Blesso et al (2012) found that regular egg consumption, associated with partial weight loss, was related to an increase in plasma carotenoids in patients with metabolic syndrome.

References

BRAZIL. Ministry of Agriculture, Livestock and Supply. Secretariat for Agricultural Defense. Meat and Derivatives Inspection Division - DICAR.Ordinance No. 01, of February 21, 1990. General Rules for the Inspection of Eggs and Egg Products. **Diàrio Oficial [da] Repùblica Federativa do** Brasil, Brasilia, DF, 6 de mar. 1990.

BRAZIL. Decree No. 56.585 of July 20, 1965. Approves the new specifications for the classification and inspection of eggs. **Official Gazette of the Federative Republic of Brazil**, Brasilia, DF, July 22, 1965.

BRAZIL. Decree No. 38.757 of January 20, 2006. Approves the regulation on the industrial and sanitary inspection of products of animal origin. **Official Gazette of the Federative Republic of Brazil**, Brasilia, DF, January 25, 2006.

BRAZIL. Decree No. 9.013, of March 29, 2017. Regulation of the Inspection Industrial E Sanitària De Produtos de Origem Animal - RIISPOA. **Official Gazette of the Federative Republic of Brazil**, Brasilia, DF, March 30, 2017.

BRAZIL. National Health Surveillance Agency. Resoluçao - RDC n° 12, de 2 de janeiro de 2001.Regulamento tècnico sobre os padrões microbiológicos para alimentos. **Official Gazette of the Federative Republic of Brazil**, Brasilia, DF, January 10, 2001.

CONRAD, Z.; JOHNSON, LK.; ROEMMICH, JN.; JUAN, W.; JAHNS, L. Time Trends and Patterns of ReportedEgg Consumption in the U.S. by Sociodemographic Characteristics. **Nutrients**, v.28, n.4, 2017.

DUMAN, M.; ŞEKEROGLU, A.; YILDIRIM, A.; ELEROGLU, H.; CAMCI, O. Relation between egg shape index and egg quality characteristics. **European Poultry Science**, n.80, 2016.

IANNOTTI, L.L.; LUTTER, C.K.; BUNN, D.A.; STEWART, C.P. Eggs: the uncracked potential for improving maternal and young child nutrition among the world's poor. **Nutrition Reviews**, v. 72, n. 6, p. 355-368, 2014.

JIA H.; HANATE, M.; AW, W; ITOH, H.; SAITO, KOBAYASHI, S.; S.; HACHIMURA,S.; FUKUDA, TOMITA, S.; M.;HASEBE, KATO, Y.; H. Eggshell membrane powder ameliorates intestinal inflammation by facilitating the restitution of epithelial injury and alleviating microbial dysbiosis. **Science Report**, v. 7, n. 43993,2017.

JAWALE, C.V.; LEE, J.H. Comparative evaluation of *SalmonellaEnteritidis* ghost vaccines with a commercial vaccine for protection against internal egg contamination with *Salmonella*. **Vaccine**, v.32, n. 45, p.5925-5930, 2014.

JONES,D.R.; ANDRESON, K.E. Housing system and laying hen strain impacts on egg microbiology. **Poultry Science**, v. 92, n. 8, p. 2221-2225, 2013.

KETTA, M.; TÛMOVÂ, E. Eggshell structure, measurements, and quality-affecting factors in laying hens: a review. **Czech Journal Animal Science**, v.61, n.7, p.299309, 2016.

LEMAHIEU, C.; BRUNEEL, C.; TERMOTE-VERHALLE,R.; MUYLAERT, K.; BUYSE, J.; FOUBERT, I. Impact of feed supplementation with different omega-3 rich microalgae species on enrichment of eggs of laying hens. **Food Chemistry**,[S.I.]: v.141, p.4051-4059,2013.

LIU, J.; JIN, Y.; LIN, S.; JONES, G.S.; CHEN, F. Purification and identification of novel antioxidant peptides from egg white protein and their antioxidant activities. **Food Chemistry**, [S.I.]: v. 175, p.258-266, 2015.

LIU, Y.C.; CHEN, WU, , T.H.; Y.C.; LEEY.C.; TAN, F.J. Effects of egg washing and storage temperature on the quality of eggshell cuticle and eggs. **FoodChemistry**, [S.I.]: v.211, p.687-689, 2016.

NANDRE, R.; MATSUDA, K.; LEE, J.H. Efficacy for a New Live Attenuated *SalmonellaEnteritidis* Vaccine Candidate to Reduce Internal Egg Contamination. **Vaccine**, v. 61, n. 1, p. 55-63, 2013.

PISKORSKA-PLISZCZYNSKA, J.; MIKOLAJCZYK, S.; WARENIK-BANY, M.; MASZEWSKI, S.; STRUCINSKI, P. Soil as a source of dioxin contamination in eggs from free-range hens on a Polish farmDLScience of the Total Environment, [S.I.]: v. 1, p.447-454, 2014.

POKORA, m.; ZAMBROWICZ, A.; D^BROWSKA, A.; ECKERT, E.; SETNER, B.; SZOETYSIK, M.; SZEWCZUK, Z.; ZABEOCKA,A.; POLANOWSKI, A.; TRZISZKA, T.; CHRZANOWSKA, J. An attractive way of egg white protein byproduct use for producing of novel anti-hypertensive peptides. **Food Chemistry**, [S.I.]: v.151, p.500-505, 2014.

REN, Y.; WU, H.; LI, X.; LAI, F.; XIAO, X. Purification and characterization of high antioxidant peptides from duck egg white protein hydrolysates. **Biochemical and Biophysical Research** Communications, v.452, n. 4, p. 888-894, 2014.

SANTINI, A.; NAVIGLIO, D.; GALLO, M.; LE GROTTAGLIE, L.; SCALA, C.; FERRARA, L. Determination of cholesterol in Italian chicken eggs. **Food Chemistry**,v.132, n. 2, p.701-708, 2012.

SHI, Z.; YUAN, B.; ZHANG, C.; ZHOU, M.; HOLMBOE-OTTESEN, G. Egg consumption and the risk of diabetes in adults, Jiangsu, China. **Nutrition**, v.27, p.194-198, 2011.

SURESH, P.V. RATHINA, K.; NIDHEESH, T.; PAL, G.K., SAKHARE, P.Z. Application of chitosan for improvement of quality and shelf life of table eggs under tropical room conditions. **Journal of Food Science Technology**, v.52, n. 10, p.63456354, 2015.

SUTHIENKUL, O.; UTRARACHKIJ, F.; PORNRAUNGWONG, S.; SIRIPANICHGON, K.; NAKAJIMA, C.; SUZUKI, Y. Possible horizontal transmission of Salmonella via reusable egg trays in Thailand. **International Journal of Food Microbiology**, v.154, n. 1-2, p.73-78, 2012.

VAIBHAV C.; GOLE, K.K.; CHOUSALKAR J.R.; SEXTON, R.M.; TAN, D.M.J.; KIERMEIER, K. Effect of Egg Washing and Correlation between Eggshell

Characteristics and Egg Penetration by Various *Salmonella typhimurium* Strains. **Plos One**, v. 9, n. 3, p. e90987, 2014.

WU, X.;TONG, Y.;SHANKAR, K;KANG, .;BAUMGARDNER, J. N.J.; BADEAUX BADGERJ.; , RONIS, T. M.; M. J. J. Lipid Fatty Acid Profile Analyses in Liver and Serum in Rats with Nonalcoholic Steatohepatitis Using Improved Gas Chromatography-Mass Spectrometry Methodology. **Journal Agricultural and Food Chemistry**,v. 59, n. 2, p. 747-754, 2011.

YUCEER, M.; CANER, C. Antimicrobial lysozyme-chitosan coatings affect functional properties and shelf life of chicken eggs during storage. **Journal of The Science of Food and Agriculture**, v.94, n. 1, p.153-162, 2013.

SAMIULLAH, K.K.; CHOUSALKAR,J.R.; ROBERTS, M.; SEXTON; MAY, D. Effects of egg shell quality and washing on *Salmonella* Infantis penetration. InternationalJournalofFoodMicrobiology, v.165, n. 2, p.77-83, 2013.

CHAPTER 2

EGG PROCESSING TECHNOLOGIES

Claudiane Magliano Queiroz Medeiros; Joao Andrade da Silva; Jéssika Rodrigues Clementino; Flavia Helena Carvalho de Mélo; Jailane de Souza Aquino

Eggs are important constituents in different food products, given the advantages they can confer on them, such as: emulsification, softness, flavor and nutritional value. The use of shelled eggs, known as egg products, can be prepared in different ways, whether chilled, frozen or dried (KUMBAR et al., 2015; TECHER et al., 2014). Compared to *fresh* eggs, powdered egg coatings have proved interesting for coating fried products because they reduce the absorption of fat from the frying process. This aspect was evaluated by Meyers and Brannan (2012) who tested coating chicken-based products and observed a reduction of up to 27% in the absorption of frying fat.

According to the Brazilian Institute of Geography and Statistics (IBGE, 2016), chicken egg production reached a record 757.51 million dozen in the 2nd quarter of 2016. Nationally, there was an increase in production of 36.05 million dozen eggs compared to the same period last year. The states with the biggest increases were Sao Paulo, Goiàs, Espirito Santo, Cearà and Mato Grosso. The state of Sao Paulo leads the ranking of egg production by Federation Units, with 29.6% of national production (IBGE, 2016).

In this way, the intense production and consumption of eggs and their by-products highlights the importance of using techniques and methods that guarantee food safety and that can minimize the losses that can occur when these products are used (TECHER et al., 2014).

Brazilian legislation recommends that before industrialization, eggs should be properly washed in water with added sanitizer, the temperature of which should be between 35° and 45°C. If chlorine-based sanitizers are used, a concentration of no more than 50 ppm should be used. The process of washing and drying the eggs must be carried out quickly but efficiently, taking care not to re-contaminate them in the following stages (BRASIL, 1990; SAMIULLAH et al, 2013).

The eggshell is the initial barrier against external contamination and research into methods of improving its integrity or maintaining its quality during the storage period is intense, as once it is damaged it becomes a gateway for the entry of various contaminating microorganisms. The use of modified pressure to identify microcracks is a technique under development, which subjects the egg to negative pressure for a short time while images of its shell are captured. The negative pressure causes possible cracks in the shell to open up, making it possible to observe them through images. The major concern is that during this process contaminating microorganisms from the shell enter the egg, since the cracks will be opened voluntarily, albeit for a very short time, around 350 milliseconds. Tests carried out with *Salmonella Typhimurium* indicated that this microorganism does not penetrate the internal structures of the egg when it is subjected to negative pressure, and tests need to be carried out with other types of microorganisms, especially *Salmonella Enteritidis* (JONES; ANDRESON; MUSGROVE, 2011; JONES et al, 2013).

Due to the thermal sensitivity of egg components and the concern about maintaining the integrity of the shell, many studies have sought to improve eggshell sanitization techniques, testing methods in isolation or in combination. The use of a combination of mild moist heat (55°C) and chlorine dioxide gas against enteric *Salmonella* showed satisfactory results when the eggs were exposed to the gas and the relative humidity was at a maximum, suggesting an alternative to conventional chemical egg sanitizing techniques.

The use of radiofrequency heating as an alternative to pasteurization has been reported to be efficient, resulting in an advantage of a 60% reduction in the time of the process to achieve similar results when using hot water. In addition, when compared to microwaves, radiofrequency has an advantage due to its greater penetration capacity, as microwaves cannot reach the yolk and still cause clouding of the egg white (PARK et al, 2017). The use of ultrasound to reduce microorganisms in eggs has also been investigated and excellent results have been obtained in reducing the microbiological contamination of eggs, especially against *Salmonella sp.* and *Staphyloccoccus spp.* (AYGUN; SERT, 2012).

Another method of preserving eggs is irradiation. However, this technology has limitations, as sensory and functional properties can be affected, and irradiation can increase the production of free radicals due to lipid peroxidation, which can reduce consumer acceptance due to altered organoleptic characteristics. In general, the ideal dose for treating liquid egg whites and yolks without affecting their chemical and sensory properties is 3 kGy of gamma irradiation at room temperature followed by storage at 4°C (KEERTHIRATHNE et al., 2017).

The use of films and coatings has been investigated and in this respect the use of synthetic polymers, polysaccharides, proteins and oils have been studied. As an example, the use of chitosan, a natural polysaccharide obtained from shrimp, crab and lobster waste, has been widely used in the food industry as an external coating to help maintain the internal atmosphere of foods and to extend their shelf life. Its use in eggs has been associated with lysozyme, a bacteriolytic enzyme found in nature and approved by regulatory bodies for use in food. Thus, the development of coating films combining the use of chitosan and lysozyme seems promising, since in addition to preserving the internal contents of the egg by hindering the loss of moisture and CO_2 to the external environment, it also provides antimicrobial properties, protecting against the invasion of microorganisms.

A lot of research has been carried out with the aim of developing suitable techniques to reduce the microbial load of the egg, among them the treatments of ultrapasteurization, pasteurization, application of hot air on the surface, as well as the combination of these with other treatment methods, however, the egg has thermally sensitive components, which prevents the application of more aggressive heat methods to minimize microbial contamination without altering its components (GEVEKE; BIGLEY; BRUNKHORST, 2017).

Pasteurization is a method characterized by the use of heat at temperatures below 100

°C, under normal atmospheric pressure, which can be produced by steam, hot water, ionizing radiation, dry heat, microwaves, among others (TECHER et al., 2014; NOBRE, LIMA, 2011). Furthermore, for whole eggs and yolks, a temperature of 60 °C is used for three minutes and for egg whites, 57 °C is used for two minutes (BRASIL, 1990).

This technique is usually used by the industry to preserve liquid egg products, due to their greater sensitivity to heat (TECHER et al., 2014). Pasteurization is applied to provide a homogeneous product and is usually carried out in heat exchangers (plates) with adjusted conditions aimed at destroying pathogenic microorganisms without affecting the functionality of their proteins. It is a thermal treatment that eliminates the vast majority of microorganisms in food, but pasteurization is not capable of eliminating spore-forming bacteria, such as those of the *Bacillus cereus* group, which can therefore lead to the deterioration of eggs and their egg products (NOBRE, LIMA, 2011; TECHER et al., 2014).

In addition to pasteurization, dehydration is another technique widely used in the industrialization of eggs and is based on the removal of free water from the product. Dehydration methods include hot air circulation dehydration, vacuum dehydration, *drum drying*, *spray* drying and *freeze* drying (MA et al. 2013). This operation is widely used in the food industry, resulting in products with good quality and low water activity that are easy to transport and store (MA et al. 2013).

The use of spray drying for heat-sensitive foods has increased, due to the fact that the exposure of materials to high temperatures is short, usually ranging from 5 to 30 seconds. Eggs are a food that is normally subjected to spray drying, but the drastic increase in surface area combined with temperatures above 60°C over several days leads to thermal denaturation of the proteins (LIU et al., 2015).

The dehydration of eggs has advantages for use in the food industry when compared to the production of *fresh* eggs, such as: hindering the development of microorganisms due to the low availability of free water, facilitating the storage process by not requiring the use of refrigeration, facilitating handling and transportation and, in addition, contributing to extending the shelf life of the product, which properly stored, dehydrated eggs can last up to a year (JESÙS et al., 2013). However, the use of methods that subject the product to high temperatures during the dehydration process can cause changes in the organoleptic and nutritional characteristics of eggs, even if this exposure is for a short period of time (JESÛS et al., 2013).

In this sense, freeze-drying, which consists of removing the water from the food without subjecting it to high temperatures, offers certain advantages, since in this dehydration technique water is sublimated from frozen products by placing them under intense vacuum, taking advantage of the thermodynamic properties of water (RAMIREZ; BELLMUND; GARDINALI, 2014). In other words, in freeze-drying, water passes from a solid state to a gaseous state under controlled conditions. Thus, among the drying methods, freeze-drying is the one that seems to best preserve the organoleptic characteristics and nutritional value of food products (JESÛS et al., 2013).

Freeze-drying has three stages: freezing, primary drying and secondary drying. During freezing, the aqueous solutions of the food are transformed into a two-phase mixture, one consisting of ice and the other of a concentrate of solutes. The food is then placed in high-vacuum chambers and, as the temperature rises and the very low pressure is maintained, the temperature required to remove the water from the food is reached by sublimation, where the water passes from the solid state directly into the gaseous state. In this way, the food is not exposed to high temperatures and consequently nutritional degradation is reduced. Primary drying is where sublimation takes place and a significant part of the heat is consumed when the molecules pass from the solid state to the gaseous state. Because of this, the temperature of the frozen food decreases, and at the end of primary dehydration it is possible to notice the temperature of the product increasing, making it close to the ambient temperature (TERRONI et al, 2011).

Secondary dehydration, also called desorption, is the process that takes place after all the ice has been removed from the food, but the food still retains a certain amount of liquid water and in order to obtain a stable product the moisture content must be reduced to around 2 to 8 %, which corresponds to the strongly bound water. This can be achieved by keeping the partially dried food in the freeze-dryer for around 2 to 6 hours, heating it from 20 to 60 °C while maintaining the vacuum, which leads to the evaporation of a large part of the residual water. Another way is to combine it with another dehydration method, due to the high cost of freeze-drying. When drying is complete, with the food still in the chamber, an inert gas must be introduced, usually nitrogen, to break the vacuum, because if air enters the chamber, the product immediately absorbs moisture (TERRONI et al, 2011).

References

AYGUN, A.; SERT, D. Effects of ultrasonic treatment on eggshell microbial activity, hatchability, tibia mineral content, and chick performance in Japanese quail (*Coturnixcoturnix japonica*) eggs. **Poultry Science**, v. 91, n. 3, p. 732-738, 2012.

BRAZIL. Ministry of Agriculture, Livestock and Supply. Secretariat for Agricultural Defense. Meat and Derivatives Inspection Division - DICAR.Ordinance No. 01, of February 21, 1990. General Rules for the Inspection of Eggs and Egg Products. **Diàrio Oficial [da] Repùblica Federativa do** Brasil, Brasilia, DF, 6 de mar. 1990.

BRAZIL. National Health Surveillance Agency. Resolution - RDC No. 12, of January 2, 2001. Technical Regulation on Microbiological Standards for Food. **Official Gazette of the Federative Republic of Brazil**, Brasilia, DF, 2001.

GEVEKE, D. J.; BIGLEY, A. B. W.; BRUNKHORST, C. D. Pasteurization of shell eggs using radio frequency heating. **Journal of Food Engineering**, [S.I.]: v.193, p.53-57, 2017.

IBGE - BRAZILIAN INSTITUTE OF GEOGRAPHY AND STATISTICS - IBGE. Available at

<ftp://ftp.ibge.gov.br/Producao_Pecuaria/Fasciculo_Indicadores_IBGE/abate-leite-couro-ovos_201602caderno.pdf> Accessed on 05 Dec. 2016.

JESÙS, M. N. de; ZANQUI, A. B.; VALDERRAMA, P.; TANAMATI, A.; MARUYAMA, S. A.; SoUZA, N. E. de; MATSUSHITA, M. Sensory and physicochemical characteristics of desserts prepared with egg products processed by freeze and spray drying. **Food Science and Technology**, Campinas, v. 33, n. 3, p. 549-

554, 2013.

JONES, D.R.; ANDRESON, K.E.; MUSGROVE, M.T. Comparison of environmental and egg microbiology associated with conventional and free-range laying hen management. **Poultry Science**, v. 90, n. 9, p. 2063-2068, 2011.

JONES,D. R.; ANDRESON, K.E. Housing system and laying hen strain impacts on egg microbiology. **Poultry Science**, v. 92, n. 8, p. 2221-2225, 2013.

KEERTHIRATHNE, T.P.; ROSS, K.; FALLOWFIELD, H. AND WHILEY, H. Reducing Risk of Salmonellosis through Egg Decontamination Processes. **International Journal Environment Research Public Health**. v.14, n.3, 2017,

KUMBAR, V.; TRNKAB, J.; NEDOMOVÂC, S.; BUCHARA, J. On the influence of storage duration on rheological properties of liquid egg products and response of eggs to impact loading - Japanese quail eggs. **Journal of Food Engineering**, [S.I.]: v. 166, p. 86-94, 2015.

LIU, L., WANG, H.; REN, G. Y.; DUAN, X.; LI, D.; YIN, G. J. Effects of freezedrying and spray drying processes on functional properties of phosphorylation of egg white protein. **International Journal of Agricultural and Biological Engineering**, [S.I.], v.8, n.4, p. 116-123, 2015.

MA, S.; ZHAO, S.; ZHANG, Y.; YU, Y.; LIU, J.; XU, M. Quality characteristic of spray-drying egg white powders. **Molecular biology Reports**, [S.I.], v. 40, n.10, p. 5677-5683, 2013.

MYERS, A.S.; BRANNAN, R.G. Efficacy of fresh and dried egg white on inhibition of oil absorption during deep fat frying. **Journal of Food Quality**, v. 35, n. 4, p. 239246, 2012.

NOBRE, J. A. S.; LIMA, D. M. **Food processing technology.** Sao Paulo: Ibemec, 2011.

PARK, S.; BEUCHAT, L.R.; KIM, H. JEE-HOON R. Inactivation of *Salmonella entericain* chicken feces on the surface of eggshells by simultaneous treatments with gaseous chlorine dioxide and mild wet heat. **Food Microbiology**, [S.I.]: v.62, p.202206, 2017.

RAMIREZ, C. E.; BELLMUND, S; GARDINALI, P. R. A simple method for routine monitoring of glyphosate and its main metabolite in surface waters using lyophilization and LC-FLD + MS/MS. Case study: canals with influence on Biscayne National Park. **Science of the Total Environment**, v. 496, p. 389-401, 2014.

SAMIULLAH, K.K.; CHOUSALKAR,J.R.; ROBERTS, M.; SEXTON; MAY, D. Effects of egg shell quality and washing on *Salmonella Infantis* penetration. **International Journal of Food Microbiology**, v.165, n. 2, p.77-83, 2013.

TECHER, C.; BARON, F.; DELBRASSINNE, L; BELAID, R.; BRUNET, N.; GILLARD, A.; GONNET, F.; COCHET, M.-F.; GROSSET, N.; GAUTIER, M.; ANDJELKOVIC, M.; LECHEVALIER, V.; JAN, S. Global overview of the risk linked to the Bacillus cereus group in the egg product industry: identification of food safety and food spoilage markers. **Journal of Applied Microbiology**, v.116, n. 5, p. 1344-1358, 2014.

TERRONI, H. C.; DE JESUS, J. M.; ARTUZO, L. T.; VENTURA, L. V.; SANTOS, R. F.; DAMY-BENEDETTI, P. Liofilizaçao. **Revista Cientifica Unilago**, v.1, p.271284, 2011.

CHAPTER 3

THE INFLUENCE OF PROCESSING ON THE FUNCTIONAL AND NUTRITIONAL PROPERTIES OF EGGS

Flavia Helena Carvalho de Mélo; Claudiane Magliano Queiroz Medeiros; Joao Andrade da Silva; Jailane de Souza Aquino

Chicken eggs contain important proteins for the human diet. In addition, the functional properties present in these proteins, such as the potential to form gels, foams and emulsions, especially those contained in the egg white, make the egg a relevant ingredient for the food industry, in addition to contributing to the organoleptic characteristics of food products, thus favoring the flavor, color and odor of the products, in addition to increasing their nutritional quality (BENEDÉ et al., 2015; ABEYRATHNE; LEE; AHN, 2013; NYEMB et al., 2014).

Egg proteins are more concentrated in the white and yolk, however, the yolk has a higher lipid content than the white (ABEYRATHNE; LEE; AHN, 2013). The main proteins found in hen's eggs are: egg albumin; egg transferrin; ovomucin; ovomucoid, avidin, lysozyme, phosvitin, among others. Some proteins are linked to carbohydrates or lipids to form glycoproteins or lipoproteins. These proteins, as well as the peptides derived from them, have important properties for human health, such as antihypertensive, antioxidant, antimicrobial and immunomodulatory functions, as well as being mineral binders. Both proteins and peptides have important characteristics for the pharmaceutical, nutraceutical and food industries (ZHIPENG et al., 2014; ABEYRATHNE; LEE; AHN, 2013).

Some of the main characteristics of egg proteins, such as ovalbumin, ovotransferrin, ovomucin, ovomucoid, isozyme and phosvitin, are listed in Table 1.

Table 1- Characteristics of the main proteins present in eggs

Protein	Features
Ovalbumin	The main protein in egg whites;

	It has gelling, foaming and emulsifying properties.
Ovotransferrin	Compared to ovalbumin, ovotransferrin is more sensitive to heat but less susceptible to surface denaturation; Iron binder; Acts as an antimicrobial agent in food.
Ovomucina	Gelling and emulsifying properties; Used in the food industry as a food preservative.
Ovomucoid	It is characterized as a heat-resistant glycoprotein.
Lysozyme	Lysozyme is one of the main bacteriolytic proteins found in egg whites. It is used as a preservative in food.
Fosvitin	Emulsifying property Found in egg yolk

Source: Abeyrathne; Lee; Ahn, 2013; Zhipeng et al., 2014

Both *fresh* and dehydrated eggs in powder form are commonly used by the food industry, however, the quality of dehydrated eggs is directly related to the drying and storage conditions used (RANNOU et al., 2013). Despite the benefits of thermal processes on food, such as the elimination or reduction of microorganisms that can be harmful to human health, these treatments can also trigger changes in the organoleptic and nutritional characteristics of dehydrated products, such as powdered eggs (HOPPE et al., 2013). In addition, heating stimulates protein denaturation, leading to random aggregation, and this process leads to changes in the protein's tertiary structure (SHIN et al., 2013).

In the study carried out by Rannou et al. (2013), they reported that a longer storage time and a temperature of 30°C caused changes in the odor of egg powder samples. A similar finding was made by Nyemb et al. (2014), who observed that changes in the physico-chemical characteristics of food products can occur as a result of the different processing stages and ways of storing food, which can lead to changes in the food matrix, as well as its digestibility.

The speed of protein digestion is related to the utilization of dietary amino acids in metabolism, i.e. amino acid bioavailability, quantities and proportions of essential amino acids are important factors in defining protein quality in a food matrix (BARBÉ et al., 2013; SARWAR GILANI; ; WU XIAOCOCKELL, 2012). The bioavailability of proteins and peptides is related to the process of crossing the intestinal mucosa and reaching the bloodstream. However, this process is influenced by some factors of physicochemical peptides and proteinssuch as molecular size, lipophilicity , and solubility, as well as factors associated with the digestion process in both the stomach and the small intestine (RENUKUNTLA et al., 2013; UDENIGWE; ALUKO, 2012).

The stability of proteins in relation to the digestion process can be modified by various factors, such as the use of stabilizers, thickeners and emulsifiers, which can alter the stability of proteins and thus lead to lower digestibility. This can be explained by the higher viscosity of the mixture, as well as the greater interaction between different types of macromolecules and lower enzymatic activity (JIMÉNEZ-SAIZ, et al., 2013).

In the study carried out by Hoppe et al. (2013), they observed that heat treatment, both under pressure and at a temperature of up to 95 ° C for 5 min, contributed to an increase in the digestibility of pepsin from egg white proteins. A similar result was reported by Barbé et al. (2013) who observed greater hydrolysis of casein and β-lactoglobulin after heat treatment at 90°C for 10 minutes. In addition, the work carried out by Nyemb et al. (2014), who investigated the digestibility of ovalbumin *in vitro* in a model that resembled gastric and small intestinal digestion in adult humans, observed that thermal processing (80°C) favored the digestibility of the protein. These results can be explained by the that increased digestibility due to protein heating may be related to greater access by digestive enzymes to their substrates (BARBÉ et al., 2013).

While Bax et al. (2012) observed an increase in meat protein digestibility when subjected to temperatures below 70°C. However, these authors reported that thermal processes at higher temperatures (100° C) favored the appearance of oxidation reactions. In other words, higher temperatures favored changes in protein structure due to oxidation processes.

Among the reactions that can occur in food, lipid oxidation is one of the most studied. It is characterized by various chemical and biochemical reactions that affect the organoleptic and nutritional characteristics of food products, as well as causing the production of toxic compounds that can have harmful consequences for health. Among the compounds formed in these reactions are lipid peroxides, malondialdehyde and cholesterol oxidation products. These products are involved in the development of cancer cells, in cell apoptosis, and can act to inactivate enzymes and cause changes in the structure of proteins (MEDINA-MEZA, BARNABA, BARBOSA-CÂNOVAS, 2014).

Because it is a monounsaturated molecule, cholesterol is susceptible to oxidation, present in food in both free and esterified form. The most widely studied sterol oxidation process in food can be intensified by the content of polyunsaturated fatty acids present in the cell membrane, heating and temperature during this process, In addition, the composition of the product, such as the degree to which lipids are present in the composition of the food, is a determining factor in the intensity of oxidation, and the shelf life and other technologies used during processing can also influence the process of cholesterol oxidation (GEORGIOU; CONSTANTINOU; KAPNISSI-CHRISTODOULOU, 2014; ANSORENA et al., 2013; ZARDETTO; BARBANTI; ROSA, 2014).

It is important to note that cholesterol is indispensable for good health, as it makes up cell membranes and plays a role in the production of hormones and bile acids, which help in the absorption of fat-soluble vitamins A, D, E and K, as well as influencing the permeability and fluidity of cell membranes (SANTINI et al., 2012; CARDENIA et al., 2013).

The so-called cholesterol oxides are the products formed from cholesterol oxidation reactions. The concentration and type of these products are related to the original oxidation process and environmental factors such as temperature, exposure to light, water activity and the presence of other molecules with antioxidant or pro-oxidant properties (CARDENIA et al., 2013). Cholesterol oxides can cause damage to health, as they can lead to cytotoxic, apoptotic and inflammatory processes, which can contribute to atherosclerotic and neurodegenerative damage (DEREWIAKA; MOLINSKA(NÉE SOSINSKA), 2015). The presence of these compounds in the human body depends on the diet and the degree of the oxidation reaction (MEDINA-MEZA, BARNABA, BARBOSA- CANOVAS, 2014).

In cholesterol oxidation processes, the first products formed are hydroperoxides, which can undergo changes and form 7α-hydroxycholesterol (7α-HC) and 7β-hydroxycholesterol (7β-HC), along with 7-ketocholesterol -KC. The latter is the most widely used marker of cholesterol degradation in food. Other factors can affect cholesterol oxidation reactions, such as the composition of the food, the presence or absence of antioxidants or proxidants, as well as reactions with proteins, carbohydrates and lipids present in the food matrix can influence the intensity of oxidation of this compound (RODRIGUEZ- ESTRADA; GARCIA- LLATAS; LAGARDA, 2014).

Methods have been studied for the analysis of cholesterol oxides in food, among the most efficient are gas chromatography and high efficiency liquid chromatography, and among the most widely used techniques for the detection and quantification of these compounds are spectrophotometry, refractive index, flame ionization and mass spectrometry (GEORGIOU; CONSTANTINOU; KAPNISSI-CHRISTODOULOU, 2014).

In food, cholesterol oxides come from cholesterol-rich foods, especially those of animal origin, such as meat products, eggs and dairy products (GEORGIOU; CONSTANTINOU; KAPNISSI-CHRISTODOULOU, 2014). Thus, eggs are foods that have a significant amount of cholesterol in their composition, so the formation of cholesterol oxides can be common in eggs and egg products (CARDENIA et al., 2013).

The nutritional and functional value, together with the sensory characteristics of eggs, has led to their use in the food industry, especially dehydrated eggs. The pasteurization, dehydration and storage processes are directly associated with the quality of egg products, as they can influence oxidation reactions, which can lead to a reduction in the nutritional value and organoleptic characteristics of these foods (MEYNIER et al., 2014). In addition, products that contain significant amounts of lipids, such as eggs and milk, can change during storage due to oxidation processes (CHUDY, PIKUL and RUDZINSKA, 2015).

In the study carried out by Zardetto; Barbanti; Rosa (2014), they observed an increase in the concentration of cholesterol oxides in fresh egg masses subjected to a greater heat treatment, obtaining a greater amount of 7-ketocholesterol in the samples analyzed. This leads to the conclusion that the cholesterol content in the food is lost as a result of the thermal process. Furthermore, Ansorena et al. (2013) observed a decrease in cholesterol and the formation of cholesterol oxides and peroxides during the heating of cholesterol *in vitro* at 180°C. Corroborating these results , Derewiaka; Molrnska(NéeSosrnska), (2015) showed that increasing the temperature and heating time intensified the loss of cholesterol, these authors obtained losses of 12.2% and 13.9% of cholesterol at 120 ° C for 30 and 180 minutes, respectively, while at a temperature of 220 ° C for 3 hours of processing the losses were between 96.0% and 99.5%. Furthermore, as a result of thermal processing, cholesterol oxides were formed (DEREWIAKA; MOLINSKA(NÉE SOSINSKA), 2015).

Foods with a high content of polyunsaturated fatty acids such as eicosapentaenoic acid (EPA) and docosahexaenoic acid (DHA) are more sensitive to lipid oxidation processes during processing and storage. In addition, hydroperoxides from polyunsaturated fatty acids can initiate cholesterol oxidation (MEDINA-MEZA, BARNABA, BARBOSA-CÂNOVAS, 2014).

The oxidation reaction of fatty acids and steroids occurs through self-oxidation or lipid peroxidation, in which the presence of a stimulating factor, such as heat, acts as a source of energy for the formation of free radicals, generating lipid oxidation products (MEDINA-MEZA; BARNABA; BARBOSA-CÂNOVAS, 2014). In this process, the first products formed are peroxides or hydroperoxides, which are unstable in nature and lead to the formation of volatile compounds, which lead to harmful changes in the structure of the food.

Controlled temperature and lighting conditions, as well as the use of specific packaging to minimize the formation of cholesterol oxides in eggs and foods containing eggs are necessary to extend the shelf life, nutritional and microbiological quality of these products.

Furthermore, the use of eggs enriched with antioxidant substances also contributes to the lipid stability of the egg and its products (CARDENIA et al., 2013).

References

ABEYRATHNE, E. D. N. S.; LEE, H. Y.; AHN, D. U. Egg white proteins and their potential use in food processing or as nutraceutical and pharmaceutical agents - A review.**Poultry Science**, v. 92, n. 12, p. 3292-3299, 2013.

ANSORENA, D; BARRIUSO, B; CARDENIA, V; ASTIASARAN, I, LERCKER, G; RODRIGUEZ-ESTRADA, M. T. Thermo-oxidation of cholesterol: effect of the unsaturation degree of the lipid matrix. **Food Chemistry**, [S.I.]: v.141, p. 2757-2764, 2013.

BARBÉ, F.; MÉNARD, O.; LE GOUAR, Y.; BUFFIÈRE, C.; FAMELART, M.H.; LAROCHE, B.; RÉMOND, D.; LE FEUNTEUN, S. The heat treatment and the gelation are strong determinants of the kinetics of milk proteins digestion and of the peripheral availability of amino acids. **Food Chemistry**, [S.I.]: v.136, p. 1203-1212, 2013.

BAX, M. L.; AUBRY, L.; FERREIRA, C.; DAUDIN, J. D.; GATELLIER, P.; RÉMOND, D.; SANTÉ-LHOUTELLIER, V. Cooking Temperature Is a Key Determinant of in Vitro Meat Protein Digestion Rate: Investigation of Underlying Mechanisms. ***Journal of Agricultural and Food Chemistry***, [S.I.]: v. 60, p. 10, p. 2569-2576, 2012.

BENEDÉ, S.; LÓPEZ-EXPÓSITO, I.; MOLINA, E.; LÓPEZ-FANDINO, R. Egg proteins as allergens and the effects of the food matrix and processing. **Food & Function**, [S.I.]: v. 6, p. 694-713, 2015.

CARDENIA, V.; RODRIGUEZ-ESTRADA, M. T.; BOSELLI, E.; LERCKERB, G.

Cholesterol photosensitized oxidation in food and biological systems. **Biochimie**, [S.I.]: v. 95, n. 3, p. 473-481, 2013.

CHUDY, S.; PIKUL, J.; RUDZINSKA, M. Effects of storage on lipid oxidation in milk and egg mixed poder. **Journal of Food and Nutrition Research**, [S.I.]: v. 54, p. 31-40, 2015.

DEREWIAKA, D.; MOLINSKA (NÉE SOSINSKA), E. Cholesterol transformations during heat treatment. **Food Chemistry**, [S.I.]: v. 171, p. 233-240, 2015.

GEORGIOU, C. A., CONSTANTINOU, M. S., KAPNISSI-CHRISTODOULOU, C. P. Sample preparation: A critical step in the analysis of cholesterol oxidation products. **Food Chemistry**, [S.I.]: v.145, p. 918-926.

HOPPE, A; JUNG, S.; PATNAIK, A.; ZEECE, M. G.Effect of high pressure treatment on egg white protein digestibility and peptide products. **Innovative Food Science & Emerging Technologies**. [S.I.]: v. 17, p. 54-62, 2013.

JIMÉNEZ-SAIZ, R.; LÓPEZ-EXPÓSITO, I.; MOLINA, E.; LÓPEZ-FANDINO, R. IgE-binding and in vitro gastrointestinal digestibility of egg allergens in the presence of polysaccharides. **Journal of Agricultural and Food Chemistry**, [S.I.]: v. 59, n. 18, (2011), p. 10044-10051, 2013.

MEDINA-MEZA, I. G.; BARNABAB, C.; BARBOSA-CÂNOVASA, G. V. Effects of high pressure processing on lipid oxidation: A review. **Innovative Food Science & Emerging Technologies**, [S.I.]: v. 22, p. 1-10, 2014.

MEYNIER, A.; LEBORGNE, C.; VIAU, M.; SCHUCK, P.; GUICHARDANTC, M.; RANNOUB, C.; ANTON, M. n-3 fatty acid enriched eggs and production of egg yolk powders: An increased risk of lipid oxidation? **Food Chemistry**, [S.I.]: v. 153, *p.* 94-100, *2014.*

NYEMB, K.; GUÉRIN-DUBIARD, C.; DUPONT, D.; JARDIN, J.; RUTHERFURD, S. M.; NAU, F. The extent of ovalbumin in vitro digestion and the nature of generated peptides are modulated by the morphology of protein aggregates. **Food Chemistry**, [S.I.]: v.157, p. 429-438, 2014.

RANNOU, C.; TEXIER, F.; MOREAU, M.; COURCOUX, P.; MEYNIER, A.; PROST, C. Odour quality of spray-dried hens' egg powders: The influence of composition, processing and storage conditions. **Food Chemistry**, [S.I.]: v.138, p. 905-914, 2013.

RENUKUNTLA, J.; VADLAPUDI, A. D.; PATEL, S.; BODDU, S. H. S.; MITRA, A. K. Approaches for enhancing oral bioavailability of peptides and proteins. **International Journal of Pharmaceutics**, [S.I.]: v. 447, n. 1-2, p. 75-93, 2013.

RODRIGUEZ-ESTRADA, M. T.; GARCIA-LLATAS, G.; LAGARDA, M. J. 7-Ketocholesterol as marker of cholesterol oxidation in model and food systems: When and how. **Biochemical and Biophysical Research Communications**, [S.I.]:v.446, n. 3, p. 792-797.

SANTINI, A.; NAVIGLIO, D.; GALLO, M.; LE GROTTAGLIE, L.; SCALA, C.; FERRARA, L. Determination of cholesterol in Italian chicken eggs. **Food Chemistry,** [S.I.]: v.132, p.701-708, 2012.

SARWAR GILANI, G.; WU XIAO, C.; COCKELL, K. A. Impact of antinutritional factors in food proteins on the digestibility of protein and the bioavailability of amino acids and on protein quality. **British Journal of Nutrition**, [S.I.]: v. 108, n. 52, p. 315-332, 2012.

SHIN, M.; LEE, J.; AHN, K.; LEE, S. I.; HAN, Y. The Influence of the Presence of Wheat Flour on the Antigenic Activities of Egg White Proteins. **Allergy Asthma Immunology Research**, [S.I.]: v. 5, n. 1, p.42-47, 2013.

UDENIGWE, C. C.; ALUKO, R. E. Food protein-derived bioactive peptides: production, processing, and potential health benefits. **Journal of Food Science**. [S.I.]: v. 77, n. 1, p. 11-24, 2012.

ZARDETTO, S.; BARBANTI, D.; ROSA, M. D. Formation of cholesterol oxidation products (COPs) and loss of cholesterol in fresh egg pasta as a function of thermal treatment processing. **FoodResearchInternational**, [S.I.]: v. 62, p. 177-182, 2014.

CHAPTER 4

evaluation of the protein and lipid quality of eggs *in vitro and in vivo* models

Thais Helena Figueiredo do Bonfim, Claudiane Magliano de Queiroz, Joao Andrade da Silva,Jailane de Souza Aquino

EVALUATION OF PROTEIN QUALITY

Protein quality analysis is an important aspect of any consideration of human protein needs. The quality of a protein is considered to lie in its physiologically available concentration of essential amino acids. Therefore, not only the quantity is important, but also the type of protein ingested, the food matrix in which the protein is consumed and the physiological state of the individual receiving it (MILLWARD et al., 2008; TRAMONTE; SANTOS, 2013).

An important issue in evaluating protein quality refers to the bioavailability or digestibility of a protein or the ability to provide metabolically available nitrogen and amino acids to tissues and organs. The food matrix in which a protein is consumed can have a significant impact on the bioavailability of amino acids for metabolic needs. Digestive losses and structural changes of amino acids are caused by numerous anti-nutritional factors in foods (FAO, 2013).

IN VITRO PROTEIN QUALITY ASSESSMENT

- Chemical score

The amino acid score determines the efficiency with which the absorbed dietary nitrogen can satisfy the requirement for indispensable amino acids at the safe level of protein intake. This is achieved by comparing the content of the limiting amino acid in the protein with its content in the standard requirement for a reference protein (WHO, 2007). It measures the content of amino acids present in a protein source and compares the values with a protein taken as a reference for children between 2 and 5 years of age (PIRES et al., 2006). Below is the equation used to calculate the EQ:

$$EQ = \frac{\text{mg of amino acid per g of N in the test protein}}{\text{mg of amino acid per g of N in the standard protein}}$$

An example of an analysis using the chemical score method is shown below (Table 2):

Table 2- Example of chemical score calculation

Amino acids	**Test food (g/100g)**	**Standard protein (g/100g)**	**Score Chemist**
Histidine	3,22	1,9	1,69
Isoleucine	2,33	2,8	0,83
Leucine	8,47	6,6	1,28
Lysine	4,20	5,8	**0,72***
Methionine + Cystine	5,63	2,5	2,25
Phenylalanine+Tyrosine	7,05	6,3	1,11
Threonine	3,52	3,4	1,04
Tryptophan	0,80	1,1	0,73
Valine	6,09	3,5	1,74

Source: CUEVAS-RODRIGUEZ et al., 2006.

Lysine: 4.20 ÷ 5.8 = 0.72

It can be seen in the example above that the protein in the test feed will be limiting in essential amino acids, as it obtained a Chemical Score < 1.0, where the primary limiting amino acid was lysine, as it obtained the lowest result in the Chemical Score and then tryptophan as the secondary limiting amino acid.

- In *vitro* digestibility

In *vitro* digestibility is also an important parameter for assessing the nutritional potential of a protein, but it can overestimate the true nutritional value as it does not take into account biologically unavailable amino acids. Digestibility represents the portion of dietary nitrogen that is available for maintenance and growth functions (AGUILAR et al, 2015).

There are several methods for analyzing *in vitro* digestibility, such as the monoenzymatic method, developed by Mauron et al. (1955) and adopted by AOAC (1975) as the official method for proteins of animal origin, the multienzymatic methods of Akeson and Stachman (1964) and Hsu et al. (1977) and finally the method based on the simulation of digestive systems, carried out by Furuya et al. (1979), which is based on the simulation of a stomach system followed by intestinal digestion *in vitro*.

EVALUATION OF PROTEIN QUALITY *IN VIVO*

The true measure of the quality of a given food protein for human use is the growth and/or metabolic balance assessment carried out on suitable subjects from the target population. However, studies cannot be carried out routinely for reasons of cost and ethics. It is therefore essential to develop *in vitro* or animal model tests that correlate well with data from human experiments carried out for each food (GILANI, 2012).

Experiments using animal models have the advantage of reflecting both the supply of essential amino acids and protein digestibility, which are two important factors when evaluating proteins. In order for dietary proteins to meet the requirements of indispensable amino acids, their potential digestibility must be considered (BOYE; WIJESINHA-BETTONI; BURLINGAME, 2012).

The main methods for assessing protein quality *in vivo* are nitrogen balance, biological value, apparent and true digestibility, protein efficiency ratio (PER), net protein ratio (NPR), net protein utilization (NPU) and ProteinDigestibilityCorrected Amino Acid Score (PDCAAS).

The diets are calculated, balanced and prepared according to the recommendations of the American Institute of Nutrition for growing rats (Figure 1) (REEVES et al., 1993), modified by the addition of the test foods, adjusting the protein and lipid values to 9.5 and 7.7%, respectively (Table 3).

Table 3 - Composition of protein, control and experimental diets formulated with powdered eggs obtained by *spray-drying* or freeze-drying.

Ingredients	Diets (g/100g)			
	A	C	OS	OL
Casein	-	11,12	-	-
Spraydryer egg	-	-	19,9	-
Freeze-dried egg	-	-	-	20,7
Soybean oil	7,55	7,58	-	-
Starch	72,6	61,18	61,11	60,42
Sugar	10	10	10	10
Mix	1	1	1	1
Vitamin				
Mineral Mix	3,5	3,5	2,79	2,68
Cellulose	5	5	5	5
Bitartrate	0,2	0,2	0,2	0,2
Hill				
Methionine	-	0,3	-	-

*A = high-protein diet; C = AIN-93 G control diet; OS = diet modified by the addition of egg powder obtained *by spray-drying;* OL = diet modified by the addition of egg powder obtained by freeze-drying. Source: direct research.

Figure 2 - Flowchart of the preparation of the control, modified by the addition of *spray-dried* whole egg, modified by the addition of freeze-dried whole egg and aproteic diets. (A) Selection of ingredients, (B) Weighing of ingredients, (C) Mixing of dry ingredients, (D) Formation of dough, (E) Settling of dough, (F) Distribution of pellets for drying in an oven at 60°C, (G) Ready-made diets, in sequence from left to right: control diet, diet made with freeze-dried egg, diet made with *spray-dried* egg and aproteic diet. Source: authors.

The methods for assessing protein quality *in vivo* are described below:

- Protein Efficiency Ratio (PER)

The Protein Efficiency Ratio was the first method adopted for routine evaluation of the quality of protein in food. The PER is a standardized method in which newly weaned rats are fed a diet containing the test protein and another group (control) a diet with casein as the protein source, establishing the relationship between the animals' weight gain and the amount of protein consumed (GILANI, 2012).

The PER is determined on the 28th day (or 14th day) of the experiment, taking into account the animal's weight gain in relation to the protein ingested. The animals in the control group consume diets with 10% protein, using casein (standard) as the protein source, and the animals in the experimental group consume a modified AIN-93G diet with the addition of the test food, which must be renewed weekly, recording the amount of food consumed. Weighing should only be done weekly for control purposes, as the initial and final weight values are what will be used for weight control (GILANI, 2012;

MARTINO et al., 2013).

To calculate this, use the expression:

$$PER = \frac{\text{Weight gain of the test group}}{\text{PTN consumed by the test group}}$$

In general, the criteria for determining the nutritional value of proteins using the PER are: > 3.5, a protein of extremely high quality; between 3 and 3.5, a protein of good quality; between 2 and 3, a protein of normal quality; and less than 2.0, a protein of low quality (SAKANAKA et al, 2000).

Table 4- Example of calculating the Protein Efficiency Ratio (PER)

Test food	**Gain test group weight (g)**	**PTN consumed by the test group (g)**	**PER**
Egg (yolk)	156 g	42,86 g	3,64

Source: Sakanaka et al., 2000.

According to the example above, we can see that for every 1 gram of protein in the egg yolk, there is a weight gain of 0.92g. Therefore, the PER value of 3.64 shows that the protein in egg yolk is of excellent quality.

- Net Protein Ratio (NPR)

A method created by Bender and Doell (1957), which measures the difference in the growth rate of rats fed a protein and protein-free diet, checking the ability of the test protein to maintain the animal's weight and promote growth, i.e. whether the protein is used for growth and maintenance. The experiment should last 10 to 14 days.

The NPR method overcomes the major weakness in the PER assay by adding the weight loss of rats fed a non-protein diet to the weight gain of rats fed the test protein. It is assumed that the protein needed to prevent weight loss in rats fed the protein diet is equivalent to the protein needed for maintenance (GILANI, 2012). The NPR is calculated using the following equation:

$$\text{NPR} = \frac{\text{Weight gain test group} + \text{weight loss aproteic group}}{\text{PTN consumed test group}}$$

- True and apparent digestibility

Digestibility is defined as the difference between the amount of nitrogen ingested and excreted, expressed as a proportion of nitrogen ingested. Digestibility can be determined in two ways: apparent and true. True digestibility is a superior measure for determining the amino acid that is absorbed from the intestine and therefore discounts the loss of fecal metabolic matter, giving a better representation of protein quality than apparent digestibility (DARRAGH; HODGKINSON, 2000). True and apparent digestibilities are calculated using the following formulas:

$$\text{DA}(\%) = \frac{\text{I} - \text{F} \times 100}{\text{I}}$$

$$\text{DV}(\%) = \frac{\text{I} - (\text{F} - \text{Fk}) \times 100}{\text{I}}$$

Where:

AD: apparent digestibility

DV: true digestibility

1: nitrogen ingested by the test group

F:fecal nitrogen of the test group

Fk: fecal nitrogen of the high-protein diet group

- Nitrogen balance

Nitrogen balance is commonly used as an index of protein nutrition and protein status and is expressed as the difference between the amount of nitrogen ingested and the amount of nitrogen excreted in feces and urine (SAKANAKA et al, 2000). The nitrogen balance is calculated using the following formula:

$$BN = I - (F + U)$$

Where:

BN: Nitrogen Balance

I: Nitrogen intake

F: Fecal nitrogen of the test group

U: Urinary nitrogen of the test group

The true nitrogen balance (NTB) includes a group of animals with a high-protein diet (nitrogen-free - NF). Below is the formula for calculating the True Nitrogen Balance:

$$BN = I - (F - Fk) - (U - Uk)$$

Where:

BN: Nitrogen Balance

I: Nitrogen intake

F: Fecal nitrogen of the test group

Fk: Fecal nitrogen of the aproteic group

U: Urinary nitrogen of the test group

Uk: Urinary nitrogen of the aproteic group

To determine faecal and urinary nitrogen content, it is necessary to house the animals individually in metabolic cages (Figure 2), specialized for certain activities, in which urine and faeces can be collected separately.

Figure 3 - Example of a metabolic cage.

Source: Thais Helena F. do Bonfim

- Biological value

The biological value is an experimental determination of the proportion of ingested protein that is incorporated into the body, representing the fraction of absorbed nitrogen that is retained by organisms to maintain tissue integrity, development and growth (ZENGIN et al., 2012).

This is a very important nutritional parameter because it is directly related to biological metabolism. It also shows the utilization rate of proteins absorbed in the body. Proteins with a biological value of 90 or more are considered good sources of nitrogen, such as whole egg protein (SAKANAKA et al., 2000). The higher the retained nitrogen (R), the better the quality of the experimental protein. It is recommended to use a group with no protein added to the diet in order to quantify nitrogen excretion from endogenous production (MARTINO et al., 2013). Below is the formula used to calculate the biological value:

$$\text{VB:} \frac{R \times 100}{A}$$

Where:

BV: biological value

R : retained nitrogen

A : absorbed nitrogen

$$\text{VB:} \frac{I - (F - Fk) - (U - Uk)}{I - (F - Fk)}$$

Where:

BV: Biological value

I: Nitrogen intake

F: Fecal nitrogen of the test group

Fk: Fecal nitrogen of the aproteic group

U: Urinary nitrogen of the test group

Uk: Urinary nitrogen of the aproteic group

- Net Protein Utilization (NPU)

Net Protein Utilization is defined as the fraction of nitrogen intake that is retained in the body, making it possible to assess the effectiveness of test proteins for the normal growth and development of the body (AGUILAR et al., 2015). It is determined on day 28 or 14 of the experiment using the carcass method. The animals are euthanized, cut open through the abdominal cavity, and the carcasses placed in aluminum containers to dry in an oven at 105°C with forced air. The carcasses are then cooled, weighed, crushed and defatted in a Soxhlet extractor for 4 to 5 hours. They are then pulverized in a blender to determine the nitrogen content retained in the carcass (COSTA et al.,

2014). The NPU is calculated using the following formula:

$$\mathbf{NPU = \frac{B - BK}{I}}$$

Where:

B: Body nitrogen of the test group

Bk: Body nitrogen of the aproteic group

1: Nitrogen intake test group

- Protein Digestibility Corrected Amino Acid Score (PDCAAS)

In 1991, the FAO/WHO recommended that the method of digestibility corrected by the amino acid score be adopted as the official method for evaluating the nutritional quality of a protein for humans, since the amino acid composition of a protein together with its actual digestibility is sufficient information to characterize a protein from a nutritional point of view (SILVA; FROTA; ARÊAS, 2012).

In calculating the PDCAAS, the limiting amino acid score (i.e. the ratio of the first limiting amino acid in one gram of the test protein to a reference protein) is multiplied by the protein digestibility, in order to assess how well the dietary protein can match the amino acid demand, and which allows the utilization of dietary protein to be predicted (FAO, 2011). The following formula is used to calculate the PDCAAS:

PDCAAS: Chemical Score (EQ) x True Digestibility (DV)

evaluation of the lipid quality of eggs

The quality of fats differs according to their origin and composition, which are directly related to their effects on human health. An important and inexpensive source of animal fat is eggs. The nutritional quality of egg fat should be assessed according to the content of saturated, monounsaturated and polyunsaturated fatty acids present (SIMCIC; STIBILJ; HOLCMAN, 2011).

Commonly, fatty acids are determined by first extracting the lipids using the Folch method (1957), followed by esterification and separation by gas chromatography and sequential identification by mass spectrometry and quantification of the fatty acid esters (LAWLOR et al., 2010; WU et al., 2011; COOREY et al., 2015) The identification of the fatty acids present in food is carried out by comparing the retention times of the methyl esters in the sample with those of the standards. For unidentified compounds, some studies use equivalent chain length values (BRAGAGNOLO; RODRIGUEZ-AMAYA, 2002).

The determination of the amount of cholesterol in eggs has been analyzed by various methods such as spectrophotometry, gas chromatography, liquid chromatography, among others, and all these methods share the same procedure for sample preparation: a saponification extraction step of total lipids and a multi-phase solvent extraction followed by purification and concentration. Santine et al (2012) state that there is variation between the results obtained, probably due to the lack of standardization of the method applied, as well as the fact that the cholesterol concentration varies according to the weight of the yolk, breed, age and diet of the birds (SANTINI et al., 2012).

The dietary composition of fatty acids, rather than dietary cholesterol, influences blood plasma cholesterol concentrations, which have an effect on human health (FARREL, 1998). Therefore, *in* addition to chemical analysis, it is important to carry out *in vivo* evaluations *in* order to determine whether or not the composition of eggs favors an increase in blood lipid parameters in animal models or in human studies.

Biochemical markers of lipids are represented by free fatty acids in serum, circulating triglycerides, lipid components of erythrocyte membranes, phospholipids or cholesterol esters, as well as adipose tissue from different sites. In studies carried out with animals and egg consumption, the main blood biomarkers for assessing the lipid profile are cholesterol and its fractions.

LDL and HDL, triglycerides are determined by spectrophotometry using appropriate commercial kits (PEARCE; CLIFTON; NOAKES, 2011; YANG et al, 2012).

References

AGUILAR, E. G.; ALBARRACiN, G. J.; UNATES, M. A.; PIOLA, H. D.; CAMINA, J. M.; ESCUDERO, N. L. Evaluation of the Nutritional Quality of the Grain Protein of New Amaranths Varieties. **Plant Foods for Human Nutrition**, v. 70, p. 21-26, 2015.

AKESON, W. R., STACHMANN, M. A., A pepsin pancreatin digest index of protein quality evaluation. **Journal of Nutrition**, v.83, p. 257-61, 1964.

ASSOCIATION OF OFFICIAL ANALYTICAL CHEMISTS (AOAC). Official methods of analysisof the Association of Official Analytical Chemists. Washington, 1975. 1094 p.

BENDER, A. E.; DOELL, B. H. Biological evaluation of proteins: a new aspect. **British Journal of Nutrition,** v. 11, n. 2, p. 140-148, 1957.

BOYE, J.; WIJESINHA-BETTONI, R.; BURLINGAME, B. Protein quality evaluation twenty years after the introduction of the protein digestibility corrected amino acid score method. **British Journal of Nutrition**, v. 108, p. S183-S211, 2012.

BRAGAGNOLO, N.; RODRIGUEZ-AMAYA, D. B. Simultaneous determination of total lipid, cholesterol and fatty acids in meat and back fat of suckling and adult pigs. **Food Chemistry**, v. 79, p. 255-260, 2002.

COOREY, R.; NOVINDA, A.; WILLIAMS, H.; JAYASENA, V. Omega-3 Fatty Acid Profile of Eggs from Laying Hens Fed Diets Supplemented with Chia, Fish Oil, and Flaxseed. **Journal of Food Science**, v. 80, n. 1, p. S180-S187, 2015.

COSTA, N. M. B., PELUZIO, M. C. G., MARTINHO, H. S. D., HENRIQUES, G. S. *Experimental Nutrition*: Theory and Practice. In: MARTINO, H. S. D., SILVA, C. O. **Avaliaçao da Qualidade Proteica**. 1 ed. Rio de Janeiro: Rubio, 2014. chap. 5.

CUEVAS-RODRIGUEZ, E.O.; VERDUGO-MONTOYA, N.M.; ANGULO-BEJARANO, P.I.; MILA'N-CARRILLO, J.; MORA-ESCOBEDO, R.; BELLO-PE'REZD, L.A.; GARZONTIZNADOE, J.A.; REYES-MORENOA, C. Nutritionalpropertiesoftempehflourfromqualityproteinmaize (*Zeamays* L.). **LWT - Food Science and Technology**, v. 39, p. 1072-1079, 2006.

DARRAGH, A. J.; HODGKINSON, S. M. Quantifying the Digestibility of Dietary Protein. **Journal of Nutrition**, v. 130, p. 1850S-1856S, 2000.

FARREL, D. J. Enrichment of hen eggs with *n-3* long-chain fatty acids and evaluation of enriched eggs in humans. **The American Journal of Clinical Nutrition**, v. 68, p. 538-544, 1998.

FOLCH, J.; LEES, M.; SLAON-STANLEY, G.N. A simple method for the isolation and purification of total lipids from animal tissues. **Journal Biologycal Chemical**, v.226, n.1, p.497-509, 1957.

FOOD AND AGRICULTURE ORGANIZATION OF THE UNITED NATIONS - FAO. Dietary protein quality evaluation in human nutrition. Italy, 2013.

FURUYA, S.; SAKAMOTO, K.; TAKAHASHI, S.; A new in vitro method for the estimation of digestibility using the intestinal fluid of the pig. **British Journal of Nutrition**, v. 41, n. 3, p. 511-20, 1979.

GILANI, G. S. Background on international activities on protein quality assessment of foods. **British Journal of Nutrition**, vol. 108, p. 168-182, 2012.

HSU, H. W., VAVAK, D. L., SATTERLEE, L. D., MILLER, G. A., A multienzyme technique for estimating protein digestibility, **Journal Food Science**, v. 42, p. 12691271, 1977.

LAWLOR, J. B.; GAUDETTE, DICKSON, N.; T.; HOUSE, J. D. Fatty acid profile and sensory characteristics of table eggs from laying hens fed diets containing microencapsulated fish oil. **Animal Feed Science and Technology**, v. 156, n. 3-4, p. 97-103, 2010.

MARTINO, H. S. D; PELUZIO, M. C. G; COSTA, N. M. B; RODRIGUES, F. C; CONTIJO, L. N. **Nutriçâo Experimental.** Viçosa: UFV, 2013.

MAURON, J., MOTTU, F., BUJARD, E., EGLI, R. H. *The availability of lysine, methionine and tryptophan in condensed milk and milk powder; in vitro digestion studies*. Archives of Biochemistry and Biophysics, v. 59, p. 433-451, 1955.

MILLWARD, D. J., LAYMAN, D. K., TOMÉ, D., SCHAAFSMA, G. Protein quality assessment: impact of expanding understanding of protein and amino acid needs for optimal health. The American Journal of Clinical Nutrition, v. 87, p. 15761581, 2008.

SANTINI, A.; NAVIGLIO, D.; GALLO, M.; LE GROTTAGLIE, L.; SCALA, C.; FERRARA, L. Determination of cholesterol in Italian chicken eggs. **Food Chemistry,** v.132, p.701-708, 2012.

PEARCE, K. L.; CLIFTON, P. M.; NOAKES, M. Egg consumption as part of an energy-restricted high-protein diet improves blood lipid and blood glucose profiles in individuals with type 2 diabetes. **British Journal of Nutrition**, v. 105, p. 584-59, 2011.

PIRES, C. V., OLIVEIRA, M. G. A, ROSA, J. C., COSTA, N. M. B. Nutritional quality and chemical score of amino acids from different protein sources. **Food Science and Technology**, v. 26, p. 179-187, 2006.

REEVES, P.G; NIELSEN, F.H.; FAHEY, G.C. AIN- 93. Purified diers for laboratory rodents: final report f the american institute of nutrition and hoe writing committee on the reformulation of the American Institute of Nutrition (AIN)-76[a] rodent diet. **The Journal of Nutrition**, v.123, p.1939-1951, 1993.

SAKANAKA, S.; KITAHATA, K.; MITSUYA, T.; GUTIERREZ, M. A.; JUNEJA, L. R.; Protein Quality Determination of Delipidated Egg-yolk. **JournalofFoodCompositionandAnalysis**, v. 13, p. 773-781, 2000.

SILVA, A. C. C., FROTA, K. M. G., ARÊAS, J. A. G. Plenary function recognized by nutrients: Protein. **International Life Sciences Institute Brasil. (Org.)**, v. 20, p. 1-16, 2012.

SIMCIC, M.; STIBILJ, V.; HOLCMAN, A. Fatty acid composition of eggs produced by the Slovenian autochthonous Styrian hen. **FoodChemistry**, v. 125, n. 3, p. 873877, 2011.

TRAMONTE, V. L. C. G., SANTOS, R. A. *Nutriçao e Metabolismo* : Nutriçao Experimental. In: TIRAPEGUI, J., CASTRO, I. A., ALVARENGA, M. L. **Experimental Models for Studying the Nutritional Value of Proteins**. Rio de

Janeiro: Guanabara Koogan, 2013. chap. 6.

WORLD HEALTH ORGANIZATION - WHO. **Protein and amino acid requirements in human nutrition**. Report of a Joint WHO/FAO/UNU Expert Consultation. Series n° 935, Geneva: WHO, 2007.

WU, X.;TONG, Y.;SHANKAR, K;KANG, .;BAUMGARDNER, J. N.J.; BADEAUX BADGERJ.; , RONIS, T. M.; M. J. J. Lipid Fatty Acid Profile Analyses in Liver and Serum in Rats with Nonalcoholic Steatohepatitis Using Improved Gas Chromatography-Mass Spectrometry Methodology. **Journal Agricultural and Food Chemistry**,v. 59, n. 2, p. 747-754, 2011.

YANG, F.; MA, M.; XU, J.; YU, X.; QIU, N. An Egg-Enriched Diet Attenuates Plasma Lipids and Mediates Cholesterol Metabolism of High-Cholesterol Fed Rats. **Lipidis**, v. 47, n. 3, p. 269-277, 2012.

ZENGIN, G.; AKTUMSEK, A.; GULER, G.; CAKMAK, Y.; GIRÓN-CALLE, J.; ALAIZ, M.; VIOQUE, J. Nutritional quality of protein in the leaves of eleven *Asphodeline species (Liliaceae)* from Turkey. **FoodChemistry**, v. 135, p. 13601364, 2012.

MIX
Papier aus verantwortungsvollen Quellen
Paper from responsible sources
FSC® C105338

Printed by Books on Demand GmbH, Norderstedt / Germany